STEP-UP
RELIGION

What do signs and symbols mean in religion?

Jean Mead

Evans

Published by Evans Brothers Limited
2A Portman Mansions
Chiltern Street
London W1U 6NR

© Evans Brothers Limited 2008

Produced for Evans Brothers Limited by
White-Thomson Publishing Ltd,
Bridgewater Business Centre,
210 High Street,
Lewes, East Sussex BN7 2NH

Printed in China by New Era Printing Co. Ltd.

Project manager: Ruth Nason

Design and illustration: Helen Nelson at
Jet the Dog

British Library Cataloguing in Publication Data

Mead, Jean

What do signs and symbols mean in
religion? - (Step-up religion)

1. Symbolism - Juvenile literature 2. Religions -
Juvenile literature

I. Title

203.7

ISBN-13: 9780237534080

Acknowledgements

The Author and Publishers are grateful to Sarah
Kemp (Immanuel and St Andrew Primary School,
Lambeth) and Pru Ruback and Janet Monahan at
the University of Hertfordshire for their advice on
this book; and to Immanuel and St Andrew Primary
School, Lambeth, the Ruback family and Jamie
Russell, members and children of Blackhorse Road
Baptist Church, Walthamstow, Bhaktivedanta Manor
School and St Albans Mosque and Islamic Centre
for their help with photographs.

Photographs are from: Alamy: cover grid tr,
pages 1 and 7b (bobo), 9 (Tim Gainey), 18 (Tibor
Bognar), 19t (Israel Images), 24r (Religious Stock),
25t (Andrew Parker), 27tl (Janine Wiedel Photo-
library); Corbis: cover grid tc, pages 6 (Hamilton
Karie/Corbis Sygma), 8 (Haruyoshi Yamaguchi);
Istockphoto: cover tr, pages 7tl (Ian Ferguson), 7tr,
16, 20b (Edward Frederick), 21; Jean Mead: cover
grid bc, pages 4t, 5t, 10, 11t, 12, 13, 14, 15, 19c,
20t, 23l, 23c, 25bl, 26cl, 26bl, 26br, 27tr, 27b;
Mike Nason: cover grid br, pages 4bl, 4br, 11b, 17,
19b, 24l, 25br; Topfoto: page 26t; White-Thomson
Picture Archive: cover grid tl and bl, pages 20c, 22,
23r (all Chris Fairclough).

Contents

What are signs and symbols? 4

Can symbols say more than words? 6

How can symbols remind us of a story? 8

How can symbols remind us of the past? 10

The symbols at a Passover meal 12

What does it mean when you say...? .14

What does it mean when the Bible says...? 16

Symbols and an invisible God 18

Symbols that show beliefs about God 20

Symbols of respect for God 22

Symbols to look for in a church 24

Symbols and signs of belonging 26

Glossary 28

For teachers and parents 30

Index 32

What are signs and symbols?

Signs give you information or instructions. Many signs are things that you see, but there are signs that you notice with your other senses. Think of some examples of signs to add to this list:

- signs that say what places or buildings are called

- traffic signs that tell drivers and pedestrians what to do or not to do

- gestures, such as a thumbs-up sign

- a whistle blow, which signals the end of a match

- the smell of smoke, a sign that something is burning

- the feel of the special pavement surface that is used in some places to show where to cross the road.

We learn to understand many signs like these in our everyday lives. Signs are usually simple, clear and easy to recognise.

Some signs have a simple picture or design on them, called a symbol. The symbol stands for something.

▲ You can make signs, called gestures, with your body. Waving is one example. Which other gestures can you think of? What do they mean?

▼ What do these symbols stand for? Where do you see them? Sometimes the colour of a symbol plays a part in what it means.

◄ The elephant symbol on this road sign stands for a zoo.

Symbols are not realistic pictures. For example, the elephant symbol for a zoo doesn't mean that the zoo only has elephants. A symbol is a simple, stylised shape that is used to represent something real.

Sometimes we can guess what a symbol means, but often we need to learn and remember what symbols stand for. Which symbols have you learnt that are used on maps?

◀ *What do these science symbols stand for? Which other symbols do you use in your school work?*

Why do we use symbols?

Often symbols are used so that people can understand them quickly, whatever language they speak. What symbols are in instructions for washing clothes or using a DVD player?

Symbols are more noticeable than just words or a name, and so they may be remembered more. Many businesses have their own symbol, called a logo. Many schools and clubs have a badge. Logos and badges are designed to show what is special about the organisation they represent.

Powerful symbols

Symbols can link to our feelings and so they have power to influence us, without us realising why. Countries use flags, and football clubs use colours, to arouse feelings of loyalty.

Think about the way brand symbols are used in advertising. A symbol called a 'swoosh', which looks like a tick, is one of the most well-known brand symbols in the world. Do you know what it advertises and what it might mean? What do you feel when you use something with a brand symbol? Discuss with your friends whether you think brands are good, or can be too powerful.

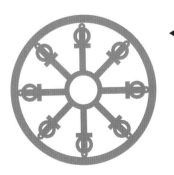

◀ *This symbol is used to represent the Buddhist religion. The eight spokes of the wheel represent a part of the Buddha's teachings called the Noble Eightfold Path.*

▼ *Which of these religious symbols do you recognise? Which religions do they represent?*

Can symbols say more than words?

Are there times when you have strong feelings but cannot find the words to say what you think? Sometimes words are not enough, and we can be 'lost for words'. Perhaps you sometimes struggle to find the right words for your feelings if you are:

- really angry
- very upset and sad
- really, really happy
- worried but you're not sure why
- amazed
- trying to say how much you love someone.

Expressing feelings

When words don't seem enough, people try to find other ways to express deep emotions. For example, taking flowers to a place can express sadness and love when someone has died.

Um, er ...

Wow!

You ... you ... ! ...

Yeah, but ...

▲ *When do people use words like these? What gestures and faces do people sometimes make when they say them?*

▶ *Many people gave flowers to show their sadness and sorrow for those who died in terrorist attacks in America in September 2001.*

▲ *Fireworks and balloons are used at special times to express joy and excitement.*

People sometimes give something to someone as a symbol of how they feel about them. A friendship bracelet is one example. A ring can be a symbol of love and commitment. Wedding rings also remind people of the promises they made to each other when they married.

Ideas and feelings in religion

In religion, people use symbols to express deep feelings and ideas that cannot be completely explained in words. A very good way to learn about religious beliefs is to investigate the symbols that are used and what they really mean to people.

▶ *In some churches, visitors can light a candle as a symbol of a prayer they make. Candles have a symbolic meaning in several religions.*

Make a card or gift

Make and give a special card or small gift, as a symbol of how you feel about your friend, parent or teacher.

How can symbols remind us of a story?

Have you seen these symbols anywhere?

rainbow   dove   olive branch

They are used to stand for:

- a promise
- peace
- hope
- beauty
- joy after misery
- gentleness
- making friends.

Which meanings go with which symbol?

The symbols of the dove, olive branch and rainbow may have begun in the Bible story about Noah's ark (right).

Noah's ark

God told Noah: 'I am going to put an end to all people, for the earth is filled with violence because of them. I am going to destroy them and everything on the earth, in a great flood. So make an ark for you and your family. Also bring into the ark a male and a female of every type of creature.' Noah did what God said and the flood began.

When the people and creatures in the ark were the only ones left alive, the flood waters gradually went down. At last, Noah sent a dove from the ark to see if it would find any dry ground. The second time Noah sent the dove, it returned with an olive leaf in its beak. The third time, the dove did not come back. Noah knew that the earth was dry again. God said that everyone and all the creatures should come out of the ark.

Noah built an altar to God, and God made a promise never to destroy the earth by flood again. God set a rainbow in the clouds and said, 'This is a sign of my promise.'

◄ Today, people sometimes release doves when they say prayers for peace.

Now, the dove, rainbow and olive branch are well-known symbols, which are used in many contexts. People may use the symbols without thinking about the story of Noah. However, knowing the story helps you to understand the symbols better and makes them more interesting.

Hindu stories and statues

Statues and pictures of Hindu gods and goddesses include many symbols. The symbols remind people of the stories that are told about the deities, such as the stories of the elephant-headed god Ganesh.

Story box

Think of a story you like. Then find objects or draw pictures that could be symbols of three important things in the story. Put them in a story box and use them to re-tell the story.

Two stories of Ganesh

Ganesh was a chubby boy made out of soap by the goddess Parvati. She gave him life and ordered him to guard her house while she bathed. When Shiva, her husband, came home and Ganesh tried to stop him going in, Shiva struck off the boy's head in rage. Parvati was so upset that Shiva grafted an elephant head on the body and gave Ganesh life again.

One day, Ganesh ate a lot of sweets. As he rode home on his mouse, In the dark, the mouse stumbled over a snake and Ganesh fell off. His over-filled stomach burst and the sweets poured out. Ganesh put the sweets back and used the snake as a belt to tie his stomach. The moon saw this and burst out laughing. Ganesh was so annoyed that he broke off his right tusk and threw it at the moon.

◀ *Hindus call Ganesh the 'remover of obstacles'. Which items from the stories above are represented in this statue of Ganesh?*

How can symbols remind us of the past?

◀ *Beth is looking at a doll that is special to her. It reminds her of her aunty Sue, who gave it to her when she was born.*

A special reminder

Think of, or bring into class, something that is special to you because it reminds you of someone or something special. Think about how it makes you feel. How would you like other people to treat it? Write a short story or draw a picture to show what it makes you think about.

An object can remind us of a story in our own lives. The object becomes a type of symbol for us, representing a special time or person.

It is not only pictures and objects that remind us of the past. A smell, a sound, a taste, the feel of something, or an activity can all wake up a lot of memories. Can you think of some examples, like the ones on the right?

I hate the smell of hospitals. It reminds me of when I was very ill.

Playing Scrabble reminds me of my friend. He always thought of amazing words!

If I eat shortbread biscuits, it reminds me of my grandma. She always made them when we went to visit.

Remembering together

Sometimes people deliberately do things together to remember past times. This can help a group of people to stay together. In the picture on the right, the bluebell walk is a type of symbol that helps the people to remember their mother and the happy times they had with her. Their feelings on the walk include both happy memories and sadness, because they miss their mother.

▶ *The women here are sisters. Each spring they go for a walk in a bluebell wood. It helps them to remember their mum, who loved bluebells.*

Poppies for remembrance

In November, many people wear poppies as a symbol of remembrance for all who have died in wars. The idea for this symbol came from a poem (right). The poem was written in the First World War, after soldiers had been killed and buried in the Flanders region of Belgium.

After the war, war memorials were built and a Remembrance Day was held each November. Paper poppies were made and sold to raise money to help former soldiers. This tradition still continues.

On page 12 you can see how symbols are used to remember a time in the history of the Jewish people.

In Flanders Fields

In Flanders fields the poppies blow
Between the crosses, row on row,
That mark our place; and in the sky
The larks, still bravely singing, fly
Scarce heard amid the guns below.

We are the dead. Short days ago
We lived, felt dawn, saw sunset glow,
Loved and were loved, and now we lie
In Flanders fields.

Take up our quarrel with the foe;
To you from failing hands we throw
The torch; be yours to hold it high.
If ye break faith with us who die
We shall not sleep, though poppies grow
In Flanders fields.

(John McCrae, 1915)

The symbols at a Passover meal

The Bible tells how, in ancient times, God rescued the Jewish people from slavery in Egypt. Jewish people remember this part of their history at the festival of Passover (called Pesach, in Hebrew). The festival begins with a meal called a seder. Some of the foods on the table are symbols. The meaning of the symbols is explained during the meal, as people read and sing the Passover service from a book called a haggadah.

◀ Matzoh are crackers made without yeast. This is the only type of bread that is eaten at Passover.

▼ Each food on the Passover plate is a symbol that helps Jewish people to remember their ancestors' experience of slavery and being freed.

Betzah is a roasted hard-boiled egg. It is a symbol of spring, as Passover is a spring festival.

Karpas is a vegetable. Parsley is often used.

Maror is bitter herbs. Horseradish is generally used.

Another type of maror.

Zeroa is a roasted shankbone of lamb. It is a symbol of the lamb that was killed on the first Passover night in Egypt. Its blood was put on the frame of Jewish houses so that the angel of death would 'pass over' them.

Charoset is a paste of apples, nuts, wine and spices.

BONE

Using the Passover service in the haggadah, the youngest child at the seder asks questions about why Passover night is different from all others. The father answers, feeling as if he was there when the Jewish people escaped from Egypt.

On all other nights we eat all kinds of vegetables or herbs. Why do we eat only bitter herbs, maror, at our seder?

The strong, bitter taste of maror reminds us of the bitter and cruel way the Pharaoh treated the Jewish people when we were slaves in Egypt.

On all other nights we eat all kinds of bread. Why do we eat only matzoh at Pesach?

On all other nights we eat sitting up straight. Why do we lean on a cushion tonight?

Matzoh remind us that, when the Jews left the slavery of Egypt, they had no time to bake their bread. They took the raw dough on their journey and baked it in the hot desert sun into hard crackers called matzoh.

We lean on a cushion to be comfortable and to remind us that once we were slaves, but now we are free.

On all other nights we don't usually dip one food into another. Why do we dip our foods twice tonight?

We dip parsley into salt water. The parsley reminds us that spring is here. The salt water reminds us of the tears of the Jewish slaves. We dip bitter herbs into charoset to remind us how hard the Jewish slaves worked in Egypt. The chopped apples and nuts look like the clay used to make the bricks for the Pharaoh's buildings.

The Passover story

Go to http://www.holidays.net/passover/story.html and read the story that is celebrated at Passover. Or read the story in a children's Bible: Exodus 12: 21-42.

What does it mean when you say...?

Words can be used in a literal way and in a non-literal way. For example, 'Pull your socks up!' can mean literally what the words say. It also has a non-literal meaning that has nothing to do with socks: get on and do better!

Non-literal expressions conjure up a vivid picture in your mind. The picture is like a symbol, which stands for the real meaning.

▼ *Here are some more non-literal expressions. What do they mean?*

I'm pulling your leg!

You let the cat out of the bag.

He's full of beans.

Keep your hair on!

He's driving me up the wall.

I was gutted.

They're over the moon.

I gave her the cold shoulder.

I saw red.

My mum hit the roof.

What's worse than raining cats and dogs?

Hailing taxis!

▲ *Some jokes are based on the idea of taking non-literal language literally.*

Non-literal language

Make a list of all the examples of non-literal language you hear or read. In a column next to them, write down what each example means. Perhaps you could make up some of your own. Have a competition in class to see who can find the most in a week, or make a class list to display.

When someone says something like this, you know that they don't mean literally that their brother is a small piece of card!

This is my baby brother.

Similes and metaphors

In literacy lessons you have probably investigated similes and metaphors. Similes compare one thing with another. They include the word 'as' or 'like'. For example:

- as white as snow

- light as a feather

- The clouds look like popcorn.

There is no 'as' or 'like' in a metaphor. When you use a metaphor, you describe something as if it were really something else. For example:

- You're a star!

- She is a pain in the neck.

Metaphors are non-literal language.

Is it true?

Non-literal language means something different from what the words say. However, this does not mean that non-literal language is not true. The word pictures of non-literal language can be true in a more subtle, powerful or interesting way than literal language. But we need to know how to interpret the word pictures. We have to understand them metaphorically.

Poets use non-literal language a lot. It is a good way to make a poem interesting and to help readers to feel a mood and emotions.

Non-literal language can be especially puzzling to understand in a foreign language. A Nigerian used a metaphor from his own language when he said about some English food, 'It is better in the mouth than in the eye.' What do you think he meant?

What does it mean when the Bible says...?

Sometimes when people read religious books, such as the Bible, they become confused because they try to understand non-literal language literally.

Metaphors in the Psalms

There is lots of non-literal language in the Bible. Especially in the Psalms, which are poems, metaphors are used to describe God. For example:

'*God is my rock.*' (Psalm 18: 2)

A rock makes us think of solid strength.

◀ Psalm 23 begins 'The Lord is my shepherd' and includes a string of metaphors to describe God. The psalm makes Christians think of Jesus, who said: 'I am the good shepherd'.

In Psalm 17, verse 8, the writer uses the following metaphor about a chick which finds safety and comfort with its mother, to describe his feeling of trust in God's care:

'*I will hide under the shadow of your wings.*'

The writer of Psalm 119 loved God's laws and teachings in the Torah. To say how the laws and teachings help him to know how to live his life, he uses this metaphor:

'*Your word is a lamp for my feet and a light for my path.*' (verse 105)

How did Jesus describe things?

The gospels show that Jesus used interesting similes when he spoke about the idea of the 'kingdom of God'. Read Mark 4: 31-32 to find what Jesus meant when he said that God's kingdom 'is like a mustard seed'.

Jesus also used metaphors, such as 'I am the good shepherd' (John 10: 11) and 'Do you look at the speck of sawdust in your brother's eye and pay no attention to the plank in your own eye?' (Matthew 7: 3-5). What did Jesus mean by that?

Parables are another type of non-literal language that Jesus used. A parable is a story or description of everyday life, which explains something else. Jesus told a parable about the joy a shepherd feels when he finds one of his sheep that was lost (Luke 15: 4-7). Jesus said that God's joy is like that when a person who has done wrong turns back to God.

Another parable is about sowing seeds. Read it, in Luke 8: 5-15, and see how Jesus said that the story was really about the different ways in which his teachings affect people's lives, depending on their attitudes.

▼ *Jesus's last supper, the night before he died, was a Passover meal similar to the one on pages 12-13. Jesus added some new symbols for his disciples. For example, when he broke the matzoh he said: 'This is my body, broken for you'. Look back at the photo on page 15 and then discuss what you think Jesus meant.*

Think about a parable

Think what Jesus was saying about God's love in the parable of the Lost Son (Luke 15: 11-31). This is often called the parable of the Prodigal Son. What does 'prodigal' mean and which part of the story is it about? Is that the most important part? What title would you give the parable?

God as 'he'

Jesus taught his followers to pray to God as 'Father', and in the Bible the pronouns 'he', 'him' and 'his' are mostly used for God. But these things do not mean literally that God is male. People believe that God is really impossible to describe in human terms, such as male and female. The English language has no suitable pronouns to use for this.

Symbols and an invisible God

Can you imagine what God looks like? Some people think of an old man with a long white beard, sitting on a cloud, but this is totally made up. People say that God is invisible, so God must be impossible to picture!

Nothing can mean something!

Muslims, Jews and some Christians think that any kind of picture of God goes against their belief in an invisible, all-powerful God. They have no pictures or statues of God or of people (especially prophets or saints) in their places of worship. This is because they think that people might worship the pictures and statues instead of worshipping God.

Mosques and synagogues are simple and plain, or decorated only with patterns and beautiful writing called calligraphy. The Arabic names for God (Allah) and the prophet Muhammad, in calligraphy, are often used to decorate the walls inside a mosque.

◀ Muslims do not use pictures or statues, but decorate their mosques with patterns and Arabic writing.

This detail shows the name of Allah. Arabic is written from right to left, so the straight line is the letter A.

In a synagogue an 'everlasting light' hangs in front of the Ark, the cupboard where the Torah scrolls are kept. The light is a symbol that God is always there.

A virtual tour

Go to http://juniors.reonline.org.uk and do a 'virtual tour' of a mosque, synagogue, or non-conformist church. Notice how few symbols you see. What clues can you find to show what is important to the people who worship there? (What is at the centre of attention, at the front?)

Non-conformist churches

There are many branches of Christianity, including several called non-conformist, such as the Baptist and Methodist churches. Many non-conformist church buildings are plain and simple, with no pictures or statues. The only symbol there is an empty cross. It stands for the belief that, although Jesus died on a cross, he is no longer dead but is alive for ever.

Some Christians belong to a group called the Society of Friends, or Quakers. Their meeting rooms are very plain indeed, just with chairs around a table. The people who go there like to sit quietly without distraction and wait for the spirit of God to guide their thoughts and speak through them.

▶ The empty cross at the front of this Baptist church shows that the death and resurrection of Jesus are very important to the worshippers.

◀ The hand at the top of this church window is a symbol for God. This symbol is used in some Jewish and Christian pictures, to show that people can know God by his actions rather than by seeing him.

Symbols that show beliefs about God

All over the world people have tried to find ways of picturing an invisible God. Because this is impossible, they have often used symbols to represent something that they believe about God.

An eternal God

Some religious symbols include a circle. A circle has no beginning and no end, and so it is used as a symbol of the belief that God is eternal.

◀ *This small banner hangs inside a car windscreen. On it is a Sikh symbol called the khanda. The circle in this symbol is called the chakar and it symbolises the perfection of God who is eternal.*

▶ *This Sikh symbol is called the Ik Onkar. It is made from the numeral '1' combined with the Punjabi word for God. It is a symbol of the belief that there is only one God.*

▶ *A Christian cross combined with a circle is called a Celtic cross. The circle is a symbol of the belief that God is eternal.*

One God

Some symbols, such as the Sikh Ik Onkar, show the belief that there is only one God.

Christians believe that God is one, but that within the one God there are three 'persons':

the Father, the Son (who is Jesus) and the Holy Spirit. This is called the Trinity. The Trinity is difficult to understand. but symbols like the ones below help to represent the 'three in one' idea.

▲ *Each of these three symbols represents the Christian idea of the Trinity. Each symbol shows the idea that the three parts of the Trinity are equal and linked together in one whole. Can you find one of these symbols in the stained glass window on page 19?*

A symbol of yourself

Make a 'diamond diagram' about yourself, showing how you are multi-faceted (for example, son, brother, football player, etc). You could include aspects of your past and possible future. Think about how you are the same person, but can be different to different people at different times. Does this help you to think about the religious beliefs that God is both one and three, or many?

Hindu beliefs

Some Hindus believe that God is one, but has many forms. There are very many Hindu gods and goddesses who are said to represent different aspects of God.

Brahma, Vishnu and Shiva are the three main Hindu gods. Brahma is the creator of the universe, Vishnu is its preserver and Shiva is its destroyer. Each of these three main gods is paired with a different goddess. For example, Shiva is paired with Parvati, the goddess of power, destruction and transformation. Ganesh (see page 9) is their son.

▶ *A Hindu belief is that the universe is created, destroyed and recreated, in an endless cycle. In this statue, Shiva is shown doing the dance of destruction to make way for a new creation. He is surrounded by a ring of fire, a symbol of destruction.*

Symbols of respect for God

Respect for God's name

One of the Ten Commandments, in the Bible and the Torah, is: 'You shall not misuse the name of the Lord your God.' For many people, this means not using the name of God as a swear word. However, some Jewish people, called Orthodox or Observant Jews, try to avoid saying the name of God at all. Instead, they use terms such as 'Ha Shem' (the Name) and 'King of the Universe'. This is similar to calling the queen 'your majesty', rather than 'Elizabeth'.

The only place where the name of God is written in Hebrew is in the Torah, but when Jews read it aloud they substitute the word 'Adonai', which is Hebrew for 'Lord'. In other writings even the English word 'God' is avoided and 'G_d' is written instead.

Gestures that show respect

Often in religion, gestures and positions of the body can be symbols of how worshippers feel about God. Bowing down is a sign of being humble (like bowing or curtseying to the queen) and is often used in worship.

Some Christians kneel and bow their heads when they pray. Muslims repeat a special series of gestures when they pray, as shown below. Can you see which of the gestures are symbols of paying attention, listening and humbly submitting to Allah?

▼ *Muslims show respect when they pray to Allah. First they get ready by having a special wash called 'wudu'. Then they stand on a clean prayer mat. As they say the prayers, they move into the positions in these pictures, so that their 'body language' shows how they submit to Allah.*

◀ *Hands held together is a symbol of prayer, but people do not always use this gesture when they pray.*

▶ Some Christians raise their hands when they pray. What do you think it means?

▲ *Hindus put their hands together and bow their heads when they approach a statue, called a murti, of one of their gods or goddesses. They show respect in the same way, and say 'Namaste', when they meet another person.*

Respect at places of worship

In their places of worship, people have symbolic ways of showing respect to God or to their holy books. When Roman Catholic Christians enter a church, they kneel down and make a gesture of 'crossing themselves', by moving their hand to touch their head, chest and two shoulders, like drawing an invisible cross.

In a gurdwara, Sikhs bow down, touching their forehead to the ground, when they approach their holy book, the Guru Granth Sahib. In a synagogue, Jewish people show their love for the Torah by kissing their fingers and touching the Torah scroll with their prayer shawl.

In some places of worship, covering the head is a sign of respect. In some, people take off their shoes. Before you visit a place of worship, you will need to find out how the people there would like you to behave respectfully.

What should visitors do?

Talk to someone who belongs to a religion and ask how he or she shows respect for God. Find out how you should behave if you visit their place of worship.

23

Symbols to look for in a church

Each branch of Christianity has its own beliefs about the use of images. This means that, when you visit churches, you will find different symbols used in different ways.

The cross is a symbol that you will find in almost every church. It is interesting to count all the places where you notice the symbol.

Non-conformist churches

On pages 18-19, we saw that there are very few symbols in some non-conformist churches. As well as an empty cross, you may find symbols of writing, such as IHS – the first three letters of Jesus's name, in Greek.

▶ *Some Christian symbols, like IHS, are made from Greek letters.*

A symbol safari

Collect photos or drawings of the symbols that you can find in your local church. Find out their meanings at http://home.att.net/~wegast/symbols/symbols.htm.

Orthodox churches

Orthodox churches have many symbols, especially icons, which are stylised pictures of Jesus, Mary and the saints. Icons stand for something more than the subject of the picture. They help people to think about Jesus, events in his life, and the saints. People kiss icons and light candles in front of them, to show that they love the person shown in the icon.

▼ *In an Orthodox church, icons like this are on the walls and on special stands. This icon shows Jesus and his mother Mary.*

Roman Catholic churches

Most Roman Catholic churches have statues and pictures of Jesus, his mother Mary and other saints. Worshippers use these to help them to pray to God.

The most important symbol is a crucifix, a cross with an image of the body of Jesus. This is usually above the altar. 'Crucifixion' means being executed on a cross, and the crucifix is a reminder that Jesus was crucified – that is, put to death on a cross.

Church of England churches

The Church of England is part of the Protestant branch of Christianity, which tries to avoid images of saints. But churches do have images of Jesus and Mary, to help people to worship. There usually is an empty cross, but often there is a picture of the crucifixion behind the altar, or in stained-glass windows. Look for symbols in carvings, wall banners, on the ceiling and in stained-glass windows. Some symbols use Greek letters because the New Testament was first written in Greek.

▲ Altars are found in Roman Catholic and Church of England churches. An altar is a table where a priest makes an offering or sacrifice to God. At the altar the priest shares bread and wine with the worshippers in remembrance of Jesus's last supper (see page 17). In the Catholic church above, the crucifix is a symbol of the Christian belief that Jesus gave up his life as a sacrifice.

▶ Christians sometimes call Jesus 'Christ'. The Chi Rho symbol is made of the first two letters of 'Christ', in Greek.

◀ This lectern where the Bible is read is in the shape of an eagle standing on a globe. An eagle stands for strength.

Symbols and signs of belonging

People sometimes show that they belong to a group by wearing a uniform, scarf or other type of clothing. Usually people feel proud to wear these symbols of belonging. Religions use symbols in this way. The symbols are worn as clothing or jewellery and displayed on cars, at home and at places of worship. Many of the symbols represent something about the religion, as well as being a sign of identity.

◀ *Except for nuns, priests and other clergy, Christians do not usually wear special clothing. A 'dog collar' (left) shows that someone is a Christian minister.*

◀ *Jewish men and boys wear skull caps when they pray.*

▶ *Some Christians use a fish symbol as a sign of their religion. In the Roman Empire, when Christians were persecuted, they used a fish symbol as a secret sign. They used a fish because the first letters of the Greek words for 'Jesus Christ God's Son Saviour' spell the Greek for 'fish'.*

▶ *Some Jewish people wear a 'star of David'. David was a king in Jewish history. In the Second World War the Nazis forced Jews to wear the star. Now they wear it with pride.*

▶ *Some Christians wear a cross or crucifix to show their faith, but other people wear crosses just as jewellery.*

Sikhs wear five symbols, known as the Five Ks. One is uncut hair. In other words, Sikhs never cut their hair. Many Sikh men wear a turban to protect their long hair. Another of the Sikh symbols is a steel bangle. Steel is a strong metal, so it reminds Sikhs to be strong. What do you think the circle shape of the bangle reminds Sikhs of?

◀

The symbol of the Muslim religion, a crescent moon and star, is used on mosque buildings.

▼

▼ These Muslims are wearing the modest dress that their religion requires.

◀ This Hindu symbol is called the 'Om'.

▲ These young people at a Hindu school have tilak marks on their faces, which show that they worship Vishnu. The girl has a dot called a bindi, which many Hindu women wear.

What do you know?

Review what you have learnt in this book. What symbols do the people on these two pages use in their places of worship? See if you know one other fact about the use of symbols in each of their religions.

27

Glossary

altar
a table of wood or stone where offerings are made to God. In a church, the altar is where the bread and wine are prepared.

ark
In the Bible story about Noah, the ark is a ship that God instructed Noah to build. In a synagogue, the ark is the cupboard in which the Torah scrolls are kept.

Baptist
a non-conformist branch of the Christian Church, in which people are baptised when they are old enough to declare their faith.

Bible
the holy book of the Christian religion. The first part of it, called the Old Testament, is almost the same as the Jewish Bible.

Buddha
the man who started the Buddhist religion when he taught people his ideas about suffering and happiness.

calligraphy
beautiful or artistic handwriting.

clergy
people who are official leaders in the Christian Church.

commitment
a serious promise; in marriage, the promise to belong to each other always.

context
the place or setting in which something occurs.

crucifix
a model or image of Jesus dying on a cross.

deities
gods and goddesses. Hindus prefer this term to 'idols'.

eternal
everlasting, with no beginning or end.

Five Ks
five symbols of appearance worn by Sikhs, which all begin with the letter K in the Punjabi language.

gestures
meaningful shapes or movements made with the body, particularly the hands.

gospel
a book in the Bible which tells the life of Jesus. There are four gospels.

haggadah
a Jewish book containing the words and the order of the seder meal.

Hebrew
the Jewish language; the language in which the Jewish Bible is written.

icon
a painted image of a holy person, which is believed itself to be holy.

Ik Onkar
the Sikh symbol meaning 'One God'.

kingdom of God
(in Christian belief) where God rules, in people's lives, or in future time.

literal
meaning exactly what it says, without interpretation.

logo
a design used by an organisation as a symbol by which it can be recognised.

memorial
something to remind people of a person who has died, or of an event in which people died.

Methodist
a non-conformist branch of the Christian Church, founded by John Wesley in the 18th century.

New Testament	the second part of the Christian Bible, which begins with the gospel accounts of the life of Jesus.
non-conformist churches	Protestant churches in England, other than the Church of England.
Observant	(of a Jewish person) especially strict about carrying out, or observing, the religious rules and customs.
olive branch	a branch of an olive tree used as a symbol of peace, or of wanting to make peace with someone.
Om	the sacred syllable that is chanted in Hindu and Buddhist prayers. It is pronounced 'ome'; and sometimes written AUM.
Orthodox	means 'right belief'; title used for a branch of Judaism and for the Eastern Orthodox branch of Christianity.
parable	a short story designed to show a moral truth.
prophet	a person who brings the message of God.
Protestant	the branch of Western Christianity that separated from Roman Catholicism in the 16th century.
psalm	a poem or song to God, found in the book of Psalms in the Bible.
Punjabi	the language of the Punjab area of India, spoken by Sikhs.
Quakers	a movement, also known as the Society of Friends, which began in Christianity, and which emphasises the spirit of God in people, rather than formal beliefs.
remembrance	the act of remembering and honouring people, things or events.
Roman Catholic	the branch of Western Christianity that regards the Pope as the head of the Church.
sacrifice	a giving up of something valuable for someone else; an offering to a god.
saint	a particularly good or holy person; usually someone believed to have gone to heaven after their death.
seder	a Jewish ceremonial meal eaten at Passover, telling the story of the escape of the Jews from Egypt.
service	a religious ceremony or meeting for worship.
stylised	made into a simple, artistic image, rather than a realistic picture.
submit	to agree to obey, humbly.
symbol	a picture, object or activity that is used to stand for, or represent, something.
Ten Commandments	in the Bible, ten laws given by God to Moses, listing how people should behave to God and to each other.
tilak	a mark made on Hindus' foreheads as a sign of the god they worship.
Torah	the most important Jewish holy book, consisting of the first five books of the Bible.
tradition	a custom that is handed down.
Trinity	in Christian belief, the idea of God being three persons in a single God.

For teachers and parents

This book is designed to support and extend the learning objectives of Unit 3A of the QCA Religious Education Scheme of Work. It includes material from Christianity and all the religions covered in most Agreed Syllabuses. The book should also be of use selectively for denominational schools exploring topics on symbolism in the context of their own religion. The content and suggested activities aim to help children to learn 'about religion' (AT1) and 'from religion' (AT2), as identified in the Non-Statutory Framework KS2 1e and 2c; and explore the specified study 3i, 'symbols and religious expression; how religious and spiritual ideas are expressed'.

Developing the skills of understanding and communicating appropriately through symbols and non-literal language is essential when encountering religions, and so this is a foundational unit for other RE topics and work on specific religions. It is also valuable in children's personal and social development. KS2 children are usually fascinated by codes and detective work, and mastery of new skills and vocabulary, so there is scope for extending the ideas in the book according to children's interest and ability. Many cross-curricular links can be made, especially with literacy, helping to integrate RE into the wider curriculum.

FURTHER INFORMATION AND ACTIVITIES

Pages 4-5 What are signs and symbols?
Focus on signs and symbols used in areas such as maths, science, history, geography, art, music, D&T, to show that each has its own 'sign language'.

'De-code' symbols such as those on instruction leaflets or mobile phones. A fun activity is to find or invent alternative translations of symbols. Humorous versions of washing symbols are on http://homepage.ntlworld.com/seanellis/b3ta/LaundryGuide.htm or http://alldaycoffee.net/story.php/83, but may need editing for children!

Investigate the symbolism of your school (or borough/county) badge.

Analyse the hidden messages in a range of logos or advertising. The Barclay's eagle symbol could link to the eagle lectern (page 25). See http://en.wikipedia.org/wiki/Swoosh about the Nike 'swoosh'.

The symbols on page 5 represent (left to right) Hinduism, Judaism, Christianity, Islam, Sikhism. Investigate their meanings and use them as headings to organise other symbols, pictures or facts for each religion.

Pages 6-7 Can symbols say more than words?
Collect and display current media pictures of events where symbols or symbolic actions are used to express feelings.

Ask the children to make friendship bracelets, for 'bracelet buddies'. This might link to the Hindu Raksha Bandhan festival, where sisters give bracelets to brothers. It can work for children in an older class to make the bracelets for 'new' children, whom they help and 'look out for'.

Try a 'guided imagery' exercise to get the class to become aware of their feelings. Let them sit in a circle around a candle. Read a 'stilling' script such as that available from www.ntlworld.com/jeanmead/re.

Pages 8-9 How can symbols remind us of a story?
Make a class collection of items or pictures with rainbow, dove and olive branch symbols.

The Noah story is in Genesis 8 and 9, up to verse 17. A similar story of Nuh is in the Qur'an (11: 25-49 and elsewhere): see www.angelfire.com/on/ummiby1/nuh.html. Differences could make it confusing to use with younger children, but be aware of it for Muslim children.

Compare story books such as *The Ark* by Pam Mara; *Stories of the Prophets from the Qur'an. Nuh (Noah)* by Siddiqa Juma; *Professor Noah's spaceship* by Brian Wildsmith. Focus on the use of the symbols.

Find stories about Ganesh and match the details to items in images of him. Photocopy an outline drawing and let the children colour in the symbols and add notes explaining them. See www.shreeganesh.com.

Pages 10-11 How can symbols remind us of the past?
Have a 'special things' session with children and staff telling about something that reminds them of a special person/time/event. Be sensitive if they are reminders of someone who has died; there is useful advice from www.winstonswish.org.uk, e.g. on making a memory box.

If you have a shared experience, such as an outing with the class, discuss what would make a good symbol to remind you all of it.

Let the children use ICT drawing software to make a personal 'heraldic shield' incorporating things that symbolise aspects of their lives.

Invite a local person to talk to the class about poppy day.

Pages 12-13 The symbols at a Passover meal
Role-play a seder, if possible with a visitor from a local Jewish family or synagogue who would bring their Passover artefacts to show and use. Or you could borrow artefacts from your RE resource centre, or build up a school resource: www.articlesoffaith.co.uk sell artefacts. Use a haggadah or information on-line to ask and answer the four questions.

At the seder Jewish people take 10 drops of wine from their glass when they read the story of the 10 plagues. Wine symbolises joy, and so this action is a symbol that their joy is lessened because others suffered. Children could draw/list the plagues and role-play this with grape juice.

Let the children draw the items of the seder plate on paper plates.

Ask children to imagine leaving home and preparing a meal that would help to bring back memories. What would they choose and why?

Pages 14-15 What does it mean when you say...?
Make links with literacy: www.standards.dfes.gov.uk/primary/
teachingresources/literacy/nls_units_of_work will provide links.

Compile an illustrated list of similes and metaphors for feelings.

Translate a poem into plain literal language and discuss what is lost.

Children could ask their families to help compile a dictionary of the non-
literal language they use, as if to help a foreign visitor.

Pages 16-17 What does it mean when the Bible says...?
REQuest (main site>bible) has a list of Jesus's parables, with Bible
references. Share these out for children to investigate, illustrate, and
discuss the meaning.

Explore similes and metaphors in the songs you use for acts of worship.

With older/more able children, discuss the different
interpretations among Christians about how far the Bible is
literally 'the Word of God'. Invite Christians to talk about
what the Bible means to them, or find statements of
belief on Church websites.

Pages 18-19 Symbols and an invisible God
In art, explore ways of trying to picture invisible things like the wind, or
qualities like goodness or anger.

Discuss why believers say that God does not have a body, but talk about
the hand/arm/heart/mouth/eyes/ears of God.

The hand of God symbol and many other Christian symbols can be
found at http://home.att.net/-wegast/symbols/symbols.htm, who will
also email high-quality line drawings for worksheets.

Pages 20-21 Symbols that show beliefs about God
Ask children to make patterns and designs using either circles or 'three-
in-one' themes. Symbols of crosses and the Trinity can be downloaded
from http://home.att.net/~wegast/symbols/symbols.htm.

Let the children investigate Sikh symbols (www.sikhs.org >Way of life >
Religious emblems), or invite a Sikh to explain the symbols.

Hindu iconography can be bewildering, and it is important to pre-empt
any tendency to be derisive. One method is to ask children to draw a
parent or carer, not to show what they really look like, but with many
arms, each showing something that the person does for them.

Pages 22-23 Symbols of respect for God
The Bible reference for the commandment is Exodus 20: 7.

Play a game where, for an afternoon, the class uses honourable titles to
address the teacher and each other. Do the register, addressing the
children as 'Adam the good listener', 'Melanie with the wonderful smile',
etc. Discuss appropriate ways of addressing the teacher.

Read the '99 Beautiful Names of Allah' at www.islamicity.com/Mosque
/99names.htm.

'Namaste' (pronounced with short 'a's as in 'nana' followed by 'steh')
originally meant 'I salute the god within you'. Discuss how the gesture
shows the Hindu belief in *atman*, the divine spirit in all living things.

Watch a video or web-clip of Muslim prayers, www.islamicity.com/
Mosque/salat/salat9.htm. Think what each body position symbolises.
Find out about wudu, head coverings and prayer mats and the
attitudes they indicate.

Pages 24-25 Symbols to look for in a church
REOnline and REQuest have links to virtual visits. Discuss why different
churches have different attitudes to imagery and symbols. Notice
whether the sacrament (altar) or the Bible (lectern or pulpit) is the
centre of attention. Link to history and the Reformation. Set children in
groups to find out about symbols in different denominations.

Draw a floor plan of a traditional Church of England church, marking
the altar and all the symbols. Show the children how it is in the form of
a cross. If you visit a church like this, a child can lie on the floor at the
crossover point and stretch their arms to demonstrate the shape.

The Chi Rho is sometimes combined with the first and last letters of the
Greek alphabet, Alpha and Omega, to show that Jesus is eternal.

Symbolic colours through the liturgical year and symbolism of clergy
clothing can be found on REQuest (Christian Symbolism >Do What).

Pages 26-27 Symbols and signs of belonging
Talk about the school uniform and other clothing or symbols that
children might wear as signs of belonging to a group. Discuss the
responsibility of being identified in this way.

If children or their family members have religious clothing or symbols
(even if not normally worn in school), ask them to show and talk about
them. Handle this sensitively, ensuring respect.

Be aware that there are diverse groups and traditions in all religions,
and help children to become sensitive to this. Also, for many people,
their affiliation to a religion is ethnic or cultural rather than actively
religious. Avoid stereotypes and generalisations by saying 'some Jews/
Christians/Muslims' etc. Make a collage for each religion, with pictures
of people and speech bubbles: 'we are all ... but we are different'.
Include 'We all don't belong to any religion, but we are different.'

USEFUL WEBSITES
QCA: www.qca.org.uk >I am interested in>Subjects>
Religious Education>Useful resources
REOnline: www.reonline.org.uk (A 'gateway' RE site with many
useful links and a child-friendly junior section.)
REQuest: www.request.org.uk (A wide range of work on Christianity.)
Parents Centre: www.parentscentre.gov.uk (Ideas for exploring
symbols and leaflets to download.)
Spirited Arts: www.natre.org.uk/spiritedarts (A gallery of children's
poetry and artwork of spiritual things, and competitions to enter.)

Index

altar 8, 25
Arabic 18
ark, Noah's 8, 9
Ark 19

badges 5
balloons 7
Baptist churches 19
belonging 26
Bible 8, 12, 13, 16, 17, 22, 25
bluebell walk 11
Brahma 21
brand symbols 5
Buddhist religion 5

calligraphy 18
candles 7, 24
Chi Rho symbol 25
Christianity, branches of 19, 24, 25
Christians 18, 20, 21, 22, 26
churches 7, 19, 23, 24, 25
  Church of England 25
  non-conformist 19, 24
  Orthodox 24
  Roman Catholic 25
circle 20, 27
clothing 26, 27
clubs 5
colours 4, 5
cross 20, 23, 24, 25, 26
  Celtic 20
  empty 19, 25

crucifix 25, 26

death 6
dog collar 26
dove 8

eagle lectern 25
emotions 6, 15

feelings 5, 6, 7, 11, 16
festival 12
fireworks 7
fish symbol 26
Five Ks 27
flags 5
flowers 6
foods 12, 13, 15
friendship bracelet 7

Ganesh 9, 21
gestures 4, 6, 22, 23
God as 'he' 17
Greek 24, 25, 26
gurdwara 23
Guru Granth Sahib 23

haggadah 12
hand symbol 19
Hindu gods and goddesses 9, 21, 23
Hindus 9, 21, 23, 27
holy books 23

icons 24
IHS 24
Ik Onkar 20

Jesus 16, 17, 19, 21, 24, 25, 26
Jewish people 11, 12, 13, 22, 23, 26
Jews 18

khanda 20

Last Supper 17, 25
light 19
literal/non-literal language 14, 15, 16, 17
logo 5
love 6, 7, 23, 24

Mary, mother of Jesus 24, 25
matzoh 12, 13, 17
memories 10, 11
metaphors 15, 16
  for God 16
Methodist churches 19
mosques 18, 19, 27
Muslims 18, 22, 27

Noah 8, 9

olive branch 8, 9

parables 17
Parvati 9, 21
Passover 12, 13, 17
places of worship 18, 23, 26
poems, poets 11, 15, 16
poppies 11

prayer mat 22
prayers 7, 8
praying 22, 23, 25, 26
Psalms 16

Quakers 19

rainbow 8
remembrance 11, 25
respect 22, 23
rings 7
Roman Catholics 23

seder 12, 13
shepherd 16, 17
Shiva 9, 21
Sikhs 23, 27
Sikh symbols 20, 27
similes 15, 16
skull caps 26
Society of Friends 19
star of David 26
stories 8, 9, 10, 17
synagogues 18, 19, 23

Torah 16, 22, 23
Trinity 21

Vishnu 21

wars 11